Arts and Crafts
You Can Eat

Also by Vicki Cobb

SCIENCE EXPERIMENTS YOU CAN EAT

HOW THE DOCTOR KNOWS YOU'RE FINE

Arts and Crafts
You Can Eat

by VICKI COBB

Illustrated by PETER LIPPMAN

J. B. LIPPINCOTT COMPANY

PHILADELPHIA AND NEW YORK

U.S. Library of Congress Cataloging in Publication Data

Cobb, Vicki.
  Arts and crafts you can eat.

  SUMMARY: Instructions for creating such artistic cuisine as mosaic
salad, cheese intaglio, carved chocolate, pasta mobile, and peach pit
ring.
  1. Cookery—Juvenile literature. 2. Handicraft—Juvenile literature.
[1. Cookery. 2. Handicraft] I. Lippman, Peter J., illus. II. Title.
TX652.5.C62   745.5   73-13864
ISBN-0-397-31491-4   ISBN-0-397-31492-2 (pbk.)

TO BEN WOLF, MY FATHER,

AN ARTIST AND CRAFTSMAN IN THE FAMILY TRADITION.

Acknowledgments

The author extends grateful appreciation to Dr. William Clark for his lesson on art history; to Ellie Haines for joining in some of the testing; to Michael Spence and his friends for making a party of snack food sculptures; to Theo and Josh, my children, and their friends Sean, Brendan, Daniel, and Tom for their help in creating more and eating less; and to my husband, Edward, for his restraint in not eating foods that were pretty enough.

Contents

Arts and Crafts
You Can Eat

1

A Kitchen Studio

Your kitchen can be an artist's studio with you as the resident artist. It has work space, good lighting, and tools you will need. The purpose of kitchen facilities is to change food so that it can be eaten. But in the process of food preparation its appearance also is changed. Knives are used to change the shapes of foods. Mixing tools change food texture. Cooking can change food shape, color, and texture. Artists, like cooks, also change the shapes, colors, and textures of their materials. But their purpose is to create something to look at. You can use food materials and kitchen facilities as an artist and create things you like to look at that are also good to eat.

Art is a way of interacting with the environment. An artist takes raw materials, such as paint and canvas, and tools, such as a palette and brush, and begins to make changes in the way materials look. (The paint and canvas are a part of the artist's environment.) He or she puts a few dabs of paint on the canvas, takes a look, and makes a decision. The appearance of the first dabs of paint helps the artist decide what the next dabs of paint should look like. Then the artist makes further changes; more paint is applied, and at each application a decision is made about the next dab of paint. Finally, there is a product—in this case a painting.

Art is a personal statement from an artist. A work of art shows the way an artist thinks about or sees something that exists. A craft is a technique or skill used by an artist to make his or her statement. Carving is the craft of making shapes by removing materials with chisels and knives. A cook might use this craft to make egg-shaped potatoes for a stew. An artist uses this craft to make pieces of sculpture.

ART AS FOOD AND FOOD AS ART

The idea of food as something pleasing to look at is not new. Cooks learn to make meals more attractive by serving food that is a balance of colors and textures on a plate. Most cooks would hesitate before serving a meal of fish fillet, mashed potatoes, and creamed cauliflower. Somehow a meal of three kinds of soft, whitish food doesn't seem very attractive, although it might be very tasty and nutritious.

Food is often used as decoration at holidays and festive occasions. Pumpkins are carved at Halloween. Fruit and nut arrangements are centerpieces on Thanksgiving tables. Decorative cookies hang on Christmas trees. Eggs are dyed and painted at Easter. Birthdays, weddings, and other celebrations feature cakes covered with drawings and sculptures. Caterers, who serve fancy food as a profession, are especially aware of the artistry involved in making food attractive, and they learn to turn vegetables into flowers and arrange canapés and hors d'oeuvres to make patterns on trays.

Food is not only good material for creating art; it is also an inspiration to artists. Bowls of fruit, feasts, and people dining have often been the subjects of paintings and sculptures. The artist's eye, trained to see beauty and meaning in ordinary aspects of life, has often seen them in food. It's reported that one famous artist thought his omelet was so beautiful he could hardly bring himself to eat it.

This brings us to an interesting point. Many people have the notion that art is something permanent—something you can keep to look at. Since you can't have your art and eat it too, art made from food is obviously not meant to be long-lasting. If you think of art only as a product, you might feel bad as you see your carefully designed mosaic salad disappear into someone's mouth. But art is more than something to look at—it's also something people *do*. Your mosaic salad can be destroyed by eating, but eating won't destroy your ability to *make* a mosaic salad. For many artists, there is more to be gained from the act of creating than from gazing at the products they have created. If you want to remember what something looked like, take a picture of it. It's probably more important to remember you can always make another.

HOW TO USE THIS BOOK

In this book we give directions for crafts. We tell you how to use syrup as paint and how to make cookies that look like stained glass windows. We give recipes for doughs you can model and bake. We also mention some of the things we made, but only as examples of how a craft can be used. We don't tell you what your project should look like. Our idea is to start you doing your own thing.

Before you begin, read through the directions and collect all your materials. Some projects require preheating the oven or making several different parts that will be assembled in the final work. Since timing is sometimes important for making good-tasting food, you should be aware of what you are going to do before you are in the middle of something and discover you missed a crucial step.

Many of the crafts are introduced with one kind of material but are suitable for use with others. Sometimes we suggest where one technique might be used elsewhere, but if you get an idea you think might work don't be afraid to try it. You can always eat your mistakes.

Every studio has its own procedures and hazards and your kitchen studio is no exception. Check with the cook in your house about rules of safety and cooking procedures before you embark on a creative adventure.

2
Drawing and Painting

Drawing is the act of expressing a thought or giving a view of nature by putting lines and shapes on a surface. It is the skill of making a hand record of things that have only existed in an artist's experience or imagination. Drawing is as important for an artist as a vocabulary is for a writer. As with many other skills, people learn to draw by observing their environment, experimenting with materials, and practicing to gain confidence and authority.

Painting is partly drawing and partly adding color and texture to drawings. The tools of the painter include the brush and palette knife. Painting techniques give artists a wider range of skills with which to express ideas than drawing alone.

The projects in this chapter involve techniques of drawing and painting with food. In order to make certain foods more suitable to an artist's purpose we often suggest the use of artificial food coloring. The natural colors of foods are often dull and not easy to extract for use in coloring other foods. Artificial food colors are clear, bright, inexpensive, and easy to use. Although they are artificial food additives, there is no evidence to suggest that they are harmful in any way.

CHOCOLATE MARSHMALLOW SCRATCHBOARD

A scratchboard is cardboard that has been coated with two layers of paint of different colors. If you draw on a scratchboard with a pointed object, the top layer of paint is removed, showing a line of the underlying color. You can make cookies into scratchboards by painting an undercoating of marshmallow topping with a thin layer of chocolate.

MATERIALS AND EQUIPMENT

2 ounces semisweet chocolate
1 tablespoon butter
large flat vanilla wafers or graham crackers
marshmallow topping
double boiler

22

knife for spreading marshmallow topping
pastry brush
spoon for stirring chocolate
paper plates for a work surface
knife with sharp point, skewer, or nail washed with soap and
    water

PROCEDURE

Put the chocolate and butter in the top of a double
boiler. Heat over boiling water until the mixture flows
easily. Don't overheat, as the solid part of the chocolate
may separate from the fat making a grainy texture.

Spread the cookies with marshmallow topping. Make
the surface as even as possible and bring the marshmallow
right to the edge. As the cookies stand, the marshmallow
topping will flow to become smooth and shiny.

Use a pastry brush to paint the melted chocolate-butter mixture on the marshmallow. Try to make the chocolate smooth and even with as few brush strokes as possible. We found a thin chocolate coat works better than a thick one. Keep the chocolate-butter mixture over warm water so it remains spreadable.

Refrigerate the cookies until the chocolate is firm—about half an hour.

Use the point of a knife, skewer, or clean nail to draw on the cookies. As you scratch away the chocolate your design will emerge as white marshmallow lines in a rich brown field.

INLAID PANCAKES

In the following project the material used to make the design is the same as that used for the background. The design is cooked longer than the background and appears dark brown embedded in a golden brown field.

MATERIALS AND EQUIPMENT

1½ cups pancake batter (1 cup mix + 1 cup milk + 1 egg)
milk
butter
knife for cutting butter
small bowl
¼ cup nesting-type measuring cup
measuring spoons
6-inch frying pan
spoon
plastic squeeze bottle with applicator tip (optional)
½ cup nesting-type measuring cup
spatula
ovenproof plate

PROCEDURE

Put ¼ cup of the pancake batter into the small bowl. Add about 1 tablespoon of milk or enough to make the batter fairly loose so it flows easily from a spoon.

Melt a teaspoon of butter in the frying pan, moving the pan around so that the surface is evenly coated. Remove the pan from the heat.

25

Draw a design on the bottom of the pan by drizzling the thinned batter from a spoon or by squeezing it from a plastic bottle with an applicator tip. (You can enlarge the hole by cutting off the end of the tip with scissors.) You can draw something recognizable or an abstract pattern.

Place your design over the heat and cook until the batter starts to brown. Quickly pour ½ cup of regular batter over the design, moving the pan so it spreads evenly. Continue cooking over low heat until the edges appear dry. Turn the pancake with a spatula and cook the other side for a few more minutes.

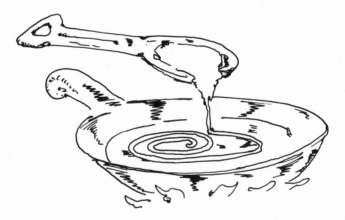

The recipe makes about three pancakes.

You can double the recipe if you wish, and you can keep finished pancakes warm on an ovenproof dish in the oven heated to 250°.

Serve with butter and maple syrup.

GIANT COOKIE PICTURE

Raw cookie dough can serve as a surface or "ground" for a painting which is then baked. The only problem is that oil or butter in the dough makes water-base paint form into a trail of small blobs wherever you pass your brush. This problem can be solved by using as the paint-base a substance that keeps water and fat from separating. One such substance, called an *emulsifier,* is soap. Soap keeps droplets of grease suspended in water when you wash the dishes.

Long ago artists discovered a natural emulsifier that also happens to be food—egg yolk. Paint pigment is mixed with egg yolk to form egg tempera, a fast drying paint used by many artists. Tempera adheres well to grounds or canvas with an oily surface. Of course, egg yolk mixed with paint pigment is no longer edible. But you can mix your own edible variation of egg tempera to use on a cookie dough ground.

MATERIALS AND EQUIPMENT

sugar cookie dough (mix your own or use the dough found in the dairy case of your supermarket)

2 eggs

food coloring
chocolate syrup (optional)
corn syrup (optional)
waxed paper
rolling pin
paring knife
cookie sheet
small bowl for egg whites
paper cups
new paintbrushes never used for paint
scissors for cutting waxed paper
spatula

PROCEDURE

Preheat the oven to 375°.

On waxed paper, roll about three tablespoons or one-third of a package of well-chilled dough into a cookie ¼ inch thick. Trim with a knife into a square 4 by 4 inches or make it a free-form shape. Trim the paper near the cookie and transfer the whole thing to a cookie sheet (greased if the cookie recipe calls for it) by flipping it upside down and peeling off the paper. Chill the cookie while you mix your "paint."

Separate the egg white from the yolk as follows. Holding an egg over a small bowl, crack it by tapping it at the center with a knife, using a swift, firm flick of your wrist. The crack should go almost around the shell.

Hold the egg in an upright position over the bowl. Gently pry the top half of the eggshell off the bottom half, letting the white slip over your hand into the bowl.

Carefully transfer the yolk from one half eggshell to the other, letting more and more egg white slip out each time. Be very careful not to break the yolk, because it is difficult to separate it from its membrane if it breaks. If it does break, start over and save the eggs for scrambling. (Note: Yolks of fresh eggs are less likely to break than yolks of old ones.)

Gently put the egg yolk, without its shell, in your left hand (or right hand if you are left-handed) and hold it over a paper cup. Give a quick jab to the yolk with a knife point so that the yolk runs out of its membrane into the cup. The membrane can make your paint lumpy.

The amount of egg yolk you use depends on how much you intend to paint. Two yolks is a good number to start with.

Divide your egg yolk into four paper cups. Make each cup a different color by adding a few drops of food coloring. Mix well with your paint brush. Clean your brush with water before putting it in a new color.

Paint your dough as you would make any painting. Then bake it until the edges turn slightly brown—about 15 minutes. Let it cool slightly before you try to remove it from the cookie sheet with a spatula.

Variations

Paint your cookie with corn-syrup-based paint mixed with coloring. This will sink into the dough during the baking process and produce a textured effect. Glaze a painted cookie before baking by painting over it with a clear coat of egg white that has been diluted with a little water.

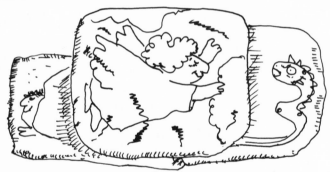

PAINTED SANDWICHES

Paint used on a porous, rough surface must flow easily. In the next project milk is the base for "paint" that can make pictures on slices of white bread.

MATERIALS AND EQUIPMENT

slices of white bread
milk
food coloring

paper cups
paintbrushes that have been used only for food
toaster

PROCEDURE

Put several tablespoons of milk into each of four paper cups. Add a few drops of food coloring to make each cup of milk a different color.

Paint the bread with your "milk paint" as you would paint any picture. We painted stripes in one direction, letting the colors blend where they overlapped, and then painted stripes at right angles to produce a plaid pattern. We also used pure food coloring directly on the bread to make strong color accents. This is a good project to experiment with different painting styles. Just be careful not to let the bread get soaked with milk.

When you have finished your painting, dry it in a toaster that is set for light toast. Use two bread paintings for a sandwich. Fill the unpainted sides with your favorite spread. You can freeze dried, painted bread to have a supply on hand. Wrap well in foil before freezing.

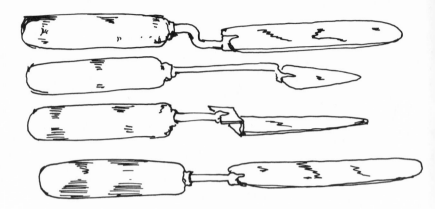

PALETTE KNIFE PAINTING

The texture of paint can add to the feeling of a painting. Many artists get different textured effects by applying paint with a flat knife instead of using a brush. Oil paints are the right consistency for the palette knife technique. Many spreads for sandwiches and hors d'oeuvres are just about the same consistency as oil paint and lend themselves well to textured, yet tasty, art.

MATERIALS AND EQUIPMENT

matzo or other large flat cracker
cream cheese
small flexible spatula or a new, clean palette knife
large white plate to use as your palette
"paints" for spreading: cheese spreads; anchovy paste; hard-
 boiled egg yolk mashed with mayonnaise; cream cheese
 blended with any of the following: green olives, pimiento,
 red caviar, paprika, turmeric, ground poppy seeds, different
 colors of food coloring, soup mixes

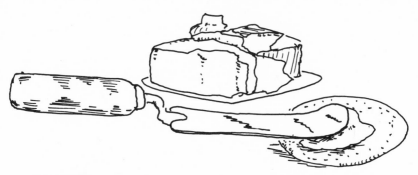

Spread the cracker with plain white cream cheese. This gives a white "ground" to your cracker surface.

Put small amounts of your various "paints" in a circle around the white plate palette. Mix colors in the center of the plate.

You can sketch a drawing in the cream cheese ground with a pointed object. Apply your "paint" by selective smearing with your palette knife. Use the tip of the knife to create different textures.

The various food spreads not only taste good but can give your painting a beautiful, muted effect of golds, browns, and reds.

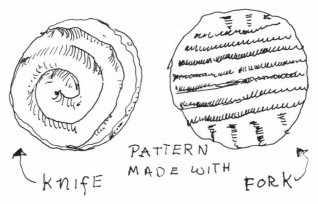

KNIFE

PATTERN MADE WITH

FORK

Every artist knows that in the course of creating a painting, accidents happen. A hand slips, paint spills on a canvas, or colors run together. Often such accidents are pleasing to the artist's eye and are left untouched to become a part of the work.

A major development in modern art came when certain artists decided that the way paint landed on canvas had a beauty all its own. Jackson Pollock dripped paint in patterns and Morris Lewis poured paint. You too can experiment with patterns and designs created by chance in the next project.

Dripped

poured

MATERIALS AND EQUIPMENT

vanilla icing (homemade or out of a can)
a plain cake or cookies
corn syrup
chocolate syrup
food coloring
paper cups
spatula
spoons

PROCEDURE

Spread the icing over the cake or cookies with the spatula. The icing is your ground. Try and make it as smooth as possible.

Pour 2 or 3 tablespoons of corn syrup into each of four paper cups. Color each with a different color of food coloring. You will have red, green, blue, and yellow. Chocolate syrup will give you brown.

Drip the syrup on the icing from spoons. Lift the cake or cookie and shift its position so the syrups run together in different patterns.

Your syrup paint will develop a "skin" and become firm on standing.

Variation

If you would like to experiment with taste as well as color, use different flavored ice cream syrups instead of colored corn syrup. Your colors can be:

yellow—pineapple syrup
amber—honey
red—raspberry syrup
brown—chocolate syrup
green—mint syrup

Spatter Pattern

3
Prints and Designs

Printing techniques are used by artists to repeat a pattern or design. An artist might want to repeat a small design, called a *motif,* many times on a single background to form an overall pattern. Examples of repeating motifs are found on wallpaper and textiles. An artist also might like to make more than one copy of a drawing that required considerable time and effort. Lithographs, etchings, silkscreen prints, and woodcuts are all examples of prints that can be reproduced many times. Each of these various printing techniques has a special quality that artists use as part of the way they express themselves.

Artists also create two-dimensional designs by arranging different materials in patterns. Stained glass is cut and embedded in lead to make beautiful windows that seem to glow when light passes through them. Another art form is mosaics, which are pictures made of arrangements of tiles, shells, or stones.

The projects in this chapter will introduce you to several different ways of producing two-dimensional designs using techniques of printing, stained glass, and mosaics, all through the use of food.

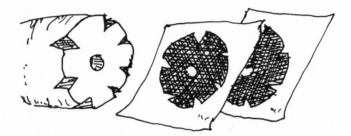

VEGETABLE STAMPS

The earliest prints, made in the fifteenth century, were playing cards. Each of the four symbols was carved on a wooden stamp. The stamps were dipped in ink and the motifs were stamped on the cards. Printing made it easy to produce playing cards in quantity. You can carve the same kind of stamp on firm vegetables.

MATERIALS AND EQUIPMENT

carrot
sharp knife
paper cups
food coloring
paper plate
sliced American cheese or peeled hard-boiled egg

Slice off the end of a carrot to produce a smooth surface. Notch all the way around the edge of the carrot and dig out a small hole in the center to form a flower design as shown in the illustration. You can also carve your initial in the carrot. The raised surface is the part that prints, and everything you cut away will not. Remember, if you carve an initial, to be sure to reverse the letter.

IHGℲƎꓷƆᗺA
ꓶꓘⁱMИOꟼÒᴚ
ƧⱿXWVUTⱿ

Pour a small amount of food coloring into a paper cup. Dip the end of your stamp in the food coloring and try out the print on the paper plate. This is to make sure you don't have too much "ink" on your stamp. Overinking blurs the edges of the design.

Stamp your design all over the white of a hard-boiled egg or a slice of American cheese. Arrange your eggs and cheese on a plate to serve.

Variations

Try making stamps out of other firm vegetables such as winter squash, potatoes, and beets. If you use beets, boil until almost tender before carving. The beet juice in the stamp can be used as ink. Simply squeeze your stamp as you press it on a surface. After several applications you may have to slice off a thin layer of the printing surface to renew your ink supply.

You can also carve a carrot to make a cylinder seal. Cut about a 1½ -inch length of unpeeled carrot that is of more or less uniform diameter. Carve shapes in its surface. Put a toothpick in each end to serve as handles. Ink the entire surface with food coloring and roll over American cheese to produce a continuous design.

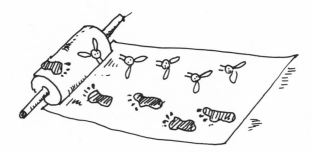

STENCILED POTATO CASSEROLE

A stencil is a cut-out pattern. It is placed on a surface and ink is passed over it. Only the cut-out areas permit the ink to reach the surface and only these areas print the design. The uncut parts of the stencil block the ink and the covered parts of the surface remain the original color.

You can make a positive stencil where the shapes you cut out will print, or you can make a negative stencil where you block out your design and ink the background. You can apply stenciled designs to all kinds of food dishes. We chose mashed potatoes because they provide a nice white ground.

The pattern is cut out

Positive stencil

Print

The background is cut out

Negative stencil

Print

MATERIALS AND EQUIPMENT

mashed potatoes in a buttered casserole (use instant mashed
  potatoes if you wish)
aluminum foil
scissors
small flexible palette knife or butter knife
pureed beets or carrots (baby food)

Cut out a piece of aluminum foil that is the same size and shape as the top of your casserole when it is folded double. Fold the foil in half two or three times. Cut out different shapes on all sides. When you open it to the double foil size you will have produced an interesting regular pattern.

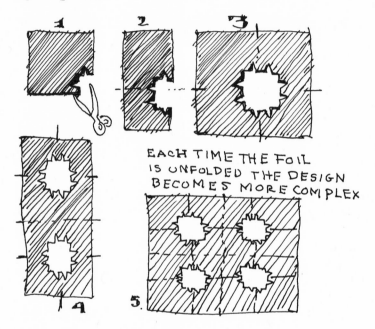

EACH TIME THE FOIL IS UNFOLDED THE DESIGN BECOMES MORE COMPLEX

Make sure the surface of the potatoes is as smooth as possible. Place your stencil on the potatoes. Carefully spread pureed beets or carrots (your "ink") over the stencil so that it fills the open spaces. Carefully lift off the stencil. The design will be printed on the surface.

Heat in a 350° oven until hot and serve.

Variations

Brush the stencil with melted butter and sprinkle with paprika or Parmesan cheese. The butter mixtures will brown more than the potatoes.

You can print catsup designs on meat loaf and jam designs on pie crusts, and sprinkle colored sugars on stencils to decorate cookies.

STAINED GLASS COOKIES

Some of the most famous works of art are the stained glass windows in major cathedrals all over the world. Panes of colored glass are held in place with lead. The technique of leading glass was also used to make household objects such as lampshades and became a popular form of art.

You can make your own "stained glass" art using cookie dough instead of lead and hard candy instead of glass. The cookies can be hung in windows or anywhere light can pass through them.

MATERIALS AND EQUIPMENT

cookie dough (recipe below)
hard candy of assorted colors (sour balls, lollipops, Charms,
    Lifesavers, etc.)

hammer
some shallow containers
waxed paper
scissors
aluminum foil
cookie sheets

Cookie Dough

Make your cookie dough preferably the day before you intend to make the cookies. The dough must chill at least two hours before it is used.

½ cup (1 bar) butter or margarine
½ cup sugar
1 egg
1¾ cups all-purpose flour
½ teaspoon baking powder
½ teaspoon salt
1 teaspoon vanilla

Soften butter in a mixing bowl, then beat until creamy. Beat in the sugar. Add all the remaining ingredients. Continue beating until dough forms. This may take 3 or 4 minutes even with an electric mixer. Cover the dough with waxed paper and chill in the refrigerator at least two hours—preferably overnight. You can easily double this recipe.

Preheat the oven to 375°.

On waxed paper, roll the dough with your hands into "ropes" about ¼ inch in diameter. Arrange the dough ropes

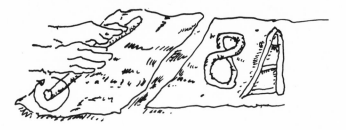

into designs on aluminum foil. The dough shapes will hold the sugar "panes." With scissors, trim the aluminum foil around each cookie so that it can be easily transferred to a cookie sheet. Bake 5 minutes for the first baking.

Remove the cookie from the oven. It should be slightly larger but not yet brown. If you want a hole to hang your cookie, make it now with a pointed object while the dough is still soft.

Put hard candy in the spaces surounded by dough. You will have to experiment to see how much to put in. We found that small broken pieces of candy were good for small spaces and that whole candies worked well for large spaces. Break the candies by wrapping them in waxed paper and banging them with a hammer. You can put only one color in a space or you can put in several colors and see how they melt together. We sorted our candy by color into shallow dishes, which made it easier to find the desired colors.

Return the cookie to the oven for about 5 more minutes. Check after 4 minutes so it doesn't overcook. A finished cookie is slightly brown and all the candy has melted.

Cool completely before trying to remove the aluminum foil. Then peel the foil from the back of the cookie rather than trying to pull the cookie off the foil.

We suggest that you try making one cookie before using your dough to make several at the same time. This is one project that may take a bit of practice before you get really spectacular results.

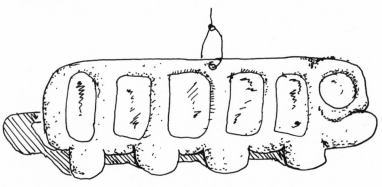

Variation

Hard candy forms as a result of the temperature to which a sugar solution is cooked. By starting with hard candy and melting it you can be sure that your finished cookie will have a hard pane. But you can get similar results by using jelly instead of candy. Like candy, jelly is a solution of sugar and water. It has not been cooked to the high temperature necessary to form hard candy. If you continue the heating process in your oven the jelly will reach the temperature necessary to form a solid pane.

Instead of baking the cookies twice, put spoonfuls of jelly in the spaces while the dough is raw. Then bake at least 10 minutes. The jelly must bubble for a while to reach the point where it will harden on cooling. It will take some experimenting to figure out the amount of jelly and the length of cooking time, but your result will be a more "natural" cookie with some interesting flavors.

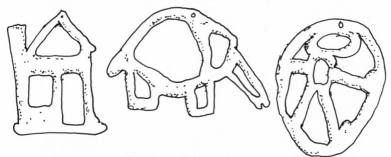

MOSAIC UPSIDE-DOWN SALAD

Mosaics are patterns made of bits of shells, stones, or glazed pottery set into cement. In this project, your "stones" are vegetables and nuts and your "cement" is gelatin dessert. The finished salad can be served with a meal as a side dish.

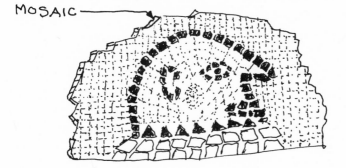

MOSAIC

2 packages of lemon gelatin dessert
vegetable "stones" (procedure below)
blanched slivered almonds
Tabasco sauce
1 cup cottage cheese
½ cup mayonnaise
cutting board
paring knife
egg beater
spoon
measuring cups
8-inch round layer cake pan (metal only)

PROCEDURE

Prepare any or all of the following vegetables as "stones" with a paring knife on a cutting board:

raw carrot, peeled and sliced crosswise
green pepper cut in strips
black olives cut in half
celery cut in small cubes
red pepper or pimiento cut in strips or cubes

Arrange a design on the bottom of the layer pan. (We made a design of carrot flowers in a cubed celery pot.) Fill in the background with slivered almonds.

Dissolve two packages of lemon gelatin dessert in 1½ cups boiling water. Add another cup of cold water and a few drops of Tabasco sauce. Carefully spoon about ½ cup of the mixture over the design in the pan. The liquid should just flow around all the vegetables or nuts so they will be held in place when it jells. If you put in too much, your design will float away.

49

Gently transfer your design to the refrigerator. Once you set down the pan, make any necessary adjustment of pieces that may have moved out of place. Also refrigerate the unused portion of the liquid gelatin.

When the unused gelatin mixture starts to thicken (in about an hour), beat in (with an egg beater) 1 cup of cottage cheese and ½ cup of mayonnaise. Pour over the design in the pan. (By this time the gelatin around the vegetables will be firm.) Chill several hours until firm.

Unmold the salad by placing the pan in hot water for about 10 seconds. This is to soften the gelatin next to the pan enough to loosen the salad. Cover the pan with a plate as shown in the picture. Invert the plate and pan and give a hard shake. Your salad should fall away from the pan. Chill until ready to serve.

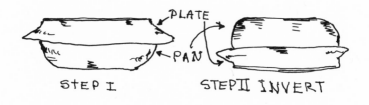

STEP I   STEP II INVERT

STEP III
SHAKE

STEP IV
REMOVE PAN

4
Modeling

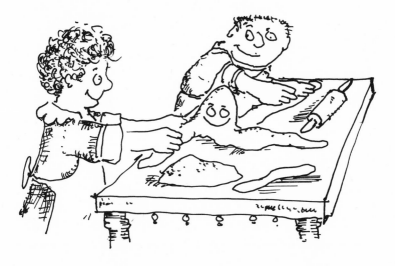

Sculpture adds a third dimension to art—depth. Artists have used many kinds of materials to create sculptures. Materials like clay and certain plastics are soft and flexible. Such materials can be made into sculpture with modeling techniques.

If you have ever modeled clay you know how to create forms by pinching, squeezing, and rolling. You may also have used tools to create textures on the surfaces as well as to press and shape the material. You can add material or you can remove it. You can build a "skeleton" for your work and then fill it in with more material.

Modeling is probably the easiest way of making designs in three dimensions. You can continually refine and correct your work without worrying about making a mistake. In this chapter you can use the modeling skills you have learned on clay to create art out of food.

MODELED MARZIPAN

Mazipan is a mixture of ground almonds (including some bitter almonds), egg white, and sugar. Long ago marzipan was eaten only by royalty but today you can buy prepared marzipan in your supermarket. If you cannot find it, buy some almond paste and follow the recipe on the can for marzipan.

Marzipan feels almost like clay with a grainy texture. Like clay, it is easily worked. Very often marzipan is modeled into shapes of different kinds of fruits, painted with food coloring, and sold commercially. Be sure your hands are clean before you start modeling.

We had fun modeling fruits and even making a marzipan bowl to put them in. We painted our fruits with food coloring which we mixed with a brush on a white plate. We also found that marzipan modeled into terrific monsters.

After painting modeled marzipan, allow the pieces to dry. Then glaze them by brushing on egg white that has been diluted with a little bit of water.

PULLED TAFFY FLOWERS

One of the skills learned by graduates of French schools of cooking is how to make flowers and bows out of sugar. Mastery of the technique is a real mark of prestige, for preparation involves an elaborate process of cooking sugar syrup to a high temperature, pouring it onto a slab of buttered marble, and folding it over and over again with a spatula. Only after it is cooled and folded many times is the sugar ready to be modeled into flower petals.

You can create the same kind of beautiful flowers with a shortcut by beginning with warm taffy.

MATERIALS AND EQUIPMENT

Turkish taffy of assorted flavors (vanilla, banana, strawberry)
double boiler
waxed paper
butter
scissors

PROCEDURE

Unwrap the taffy and place a few pieces in the top of a double boiler over hot water until soft. You can hasten the process by pushing the candy around in the bottom of the pot. The candy should be soft but not too hot to handle.

Butter the index fingers and thumbs of both hands. Pinch off a piece of warm taffy. Squeeze and stretch the candy, passing it from one hand to the other to form a flat thin "petal" that is rounded on at least one side. Lay the petal to rest on the waxed paper.

Another way to make petals is to place a small piece of taffy in a buttered spot on the palm of one hand. Then press the taffy into a round shape with the buttered thumb of your other hand.

Make at least six petals of the same flavor to form one flower. Make the flower center from another flavor of a different color. A strawberry (pink) flower might have a banana (yellow) center. To make the center, roll a small piece of taffy on a waxed paper surface.

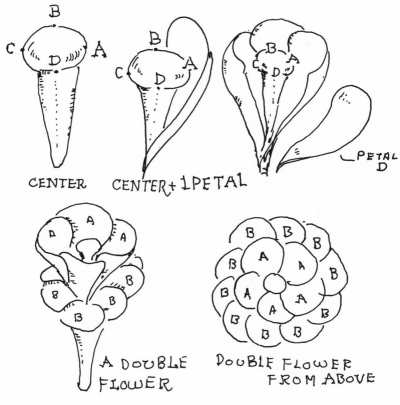

CENTER   CENTER + 1 PETAL   PETAL D

A DOUBLE FLOWER   DOUBLE FLOWER FROM ABOVE

To assemble the flower, wrap a petal around the center and pinch the bottom to hold in place. Add other petals, wrapping them around at the base. Push the petals apart to create flowers with a wider bloom. Trim away extra candy at the base with scissors.

Refrigerate finished flowers so they keep their shape. Use them to decorate cakes or the structure in sweets on p. 111. Or serve them as a bouquet using toothpicks as stems.

Chocolate
Vanilla
Strawberry

We found that warm taffy could also be modeled to make ribbons of more than one color. Just pull three flavors together. You can also make prehistoric-looking dragons.

SCULPTED DUCHESS POTATOES

Master chefs often serve mashed potatoes in elaborate fancy forms. The recipe for potatoes most easily worked is called duchess potatoes. It is similar in consistency to wet plaster—a material often used by artists. Of course, mashed potatoes don't harden like plaster but remain deliciously edible.

MATERIALS AND EQUIPMENT

instant mashed potatoes
2 egg yolks
milk
water
saucepan   } optional
wire whisk or large fork
buttered baking dish
food paintbrush
modeling tools such as a knife, fork, spoon, spatula, and anything else you might think of

PROCEDURE

Follow the directions on the instant mashed potatoes box to make four servings. (If you wish, you can wash and peel four potatoes. Cut them in quarters and boil in salted water to cover until fork-tender. Drain and mash. Beat in 2 tablespoons of butter and enough milk to make a fluffy, smooth mixture.) Let cool slightly then beat in two egg yolks. (To separate eggs, see page 28.) The egg yolks are the ingredient that makes mashed potatoes into duchess potatoes.

The potatoes are too soft to make large free-standing sculptures. We put them in a baking dish and used a knife as a modeling tool to turn our duchess potatoes into a duchess. She looked like this:

Experiment with different forms and textures. Duchess potatoes can also be shaped by extrusion molding techniques used in cake decoration. (See p. 78.)

Paint your sculpture with beaten egg which becomes shiny brown when baked, or sprinkle with paprika. Bake in a 350° oven for 30 minutes and serve.

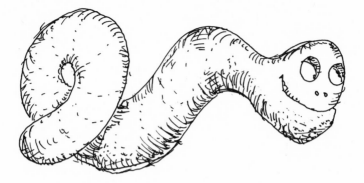

PRETZEL DOUGH SNAKES, SERPENTS, AND OTHER CREATURES

Bread dough has a marvelous feel to it. It is flexible and smooth and elastic. It has been used by artists as clay. Shapes are modeled from kneaded flour and water dough made without yeast and then allowed to dry. The product, which is hard and tasteless, is then painted and shellacked. Naturally, this kind of bread dough art is not meant to be eaten.

In order to make bread dough sculpture that is good to eat, you must use yeast, which creates problems for the artist. Yeast makes the dough rise before baking, and baking makes it expand further. The expansion process causes any fine detail of the work to be lost. You can get around this problem by keeping your pretzel dough sculpture very simple.

MATERIALS AND EQUIPMENT

1 cup warm water
1 package dry yeast
1 teaspoon sugar

1 teaspoon salt
3½ cups all-purpose flour
1 egg
coarse (kosher) salt
vegetable oil
caraway seeds or poppy seeds
large mixing bowl
electric beater or egg beater
damp dish towel
pastry brush
fork and bowl for beating egg
greased cookie sheets

PROCEDURE

Put the water, yeast, sugar, salt, and 1 cup of flour in a large bowl. Beat slowly at first, then at high speed until smooth. Make a mound of 2½ cups of flour on a clean work surface. Push in the top of the mound to make a shape like a volcano. Pour the flour-water mixture into the center of the mound. Carefully blend the flour into the liquid, using your fingers to draw in the flour.

When all the flour has been blended, knead the dough

for 10 minutes. To knead, fold the dough toward you, then push down with the heel of your hand. Turn the dough one quarter turn and repeat the motion. Flour the work surface and your hands if the mixture is too sticky at the start. As you knead, the dough will become less and less sticky. When you have finished it will be smooth and elastic.

Put the dough in a large, oiled bowl and cover it with a damp dish towel. Put the bowl in a warm place (such as the pot closet next to a heated oven) to rise until double in size—at least one hour.

Preheat the oven to 475°.

Punch the dough down. It is now ready to be modeled into anything you wish. We made sea serpents, snakes, and eels. Use caraway or poppy seeds for eyes. Place your finished sculptures well apart on a greased cookie sheet. Brush on egg that has been beaten with about a tablespoon of water and sprinkle with coarse salt. Let rise until almost double in size before baking. Bake about 15 minutes until golden brown.

GINGERBREAD STICK PUPPET

Gingerbread is one of the most widely used materials for making decorative cookies and structures. We decided to use it to make stick puppets that are entirely edible. Real stick puppets are a toy of Mexican children. They are made of wood and painted bright colors. Gingerbread stick puppets make a fun gift for young friends.

MATERIALS AND EQUIPMENT

gingerbread dough (recipe below)
shoestring licorice (black or red)
paper
pencil
scissors
waxed paper
rolling pin
paring knife and other modeling tools
colored candies for cookie decoration
raisins and nuts for decoration (optional)
cookie sheets
spatula

Gingerbread Dough

½ cup (1 bar) margarine
1 teaspoon ginger
¼ teaspoon ground cloves
½ teaspoon cinnamon
½ cup brown sugar

1 teaspoon salt
½ teaspoon baking powder
1 teaspoon baking soda
½ cup honey
⅓ cup water
3½ cups sifted all-purpose flour

Sift, then measure flour, then resift into a bowl. Set aside.

Put the margarine, ginger, cloves, cinnamon, brown sugar, salt, baking powder, and baking soda into another bowl. Mix at low speed with an electric mixer until blended.

Mix the honey and water in a small bowl. Add the flour in three parts to the margarine mixture, alternating with the honey-water mixture. Mix at low speed until a stiff dough is formed. If the dough is sticky, refrigerate for a while.

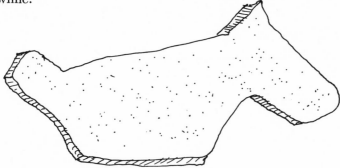

PROCEDURE

Draw a pattern for your puppet on paper. Make a simple outline of some animal, leaving off the legs, that is about 6 inches long and 2½ inches high. Cut out your pattern.

Preheat the oven to 375°.

On waxed paper, roll out a handful of gingerbread dough

so that it is about ¼ inch thick. Place your pattern on the dough and carefully cut around it with a knife. Remove the surrounding dough and gently transfer your puppet cookie to an ungreased cookie sheet. Gingerbread dough can be handled a great deal, so don't be afraid to roll it out again if you don't succeed in making a perfect cookie the first time. Any cookie you bake should be free of cracks or tears.

To make legs, cut a gingerbread rectangle 2 inches high and several inches long. Make the legs about ⅝ inch wide as shown. Make at least six legs. You need at least four for one puppet and it is a good idea to make a few extras in case there is breakage.

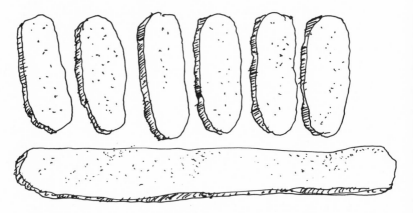

The stick on which the puppet moves is about 7 inches long and ¾ inch wide. You can form it by rolling dough with your hand and flattening it with the rolling pin or you can roll out some dough slightly thicker than ¼ inch and cut it out with a knife. Transfer legs and stick to the cookie sheet leaving space between them.

Work a design into your puppet cookie. You can model lines and textures with modeling tools and you can press in colored candies and other cake decorations. Make two small holes about 2 inches apart in the body where you will attach the legs. The holes should be about ⅜ inch above the bottom of the animal. They will close during baking but will leave marks for you to enlarge later.

Bake at 375° for about 10 minutes. Cookies will be slightly brown around the edges.

The puppet is assembled through holes in the body, legs, and stick. The time to start making the holes is when the cookies are hot from the oven. With a sharp object, such as a knife tip or skewer, make a hole in each end of each leg, and two holes in the stick about 2 inches apart. Enlarge the holes you started in the body. When the cookies are cool, they become firm. You can then enlarge the holes by rotating a knife tip in them. The finished holes should be large enough for shoestring licorice.

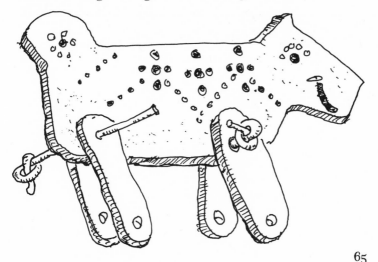

To assemble the puppet, tie a knot in one end of a piece of shoestring licorice. Thread the other end through a leg, the body, and a second leg. Make a single knot in the licorice close to the leg and trim the candy with scissors. Repeat the procedure for the second pair of legs. To mount the puppet on the stick, thread the licorice through a leg, the hole in the stick, and the second leg. Knot both sides close to the cookie and trim. Repeat the procedure for the second pair of legs.

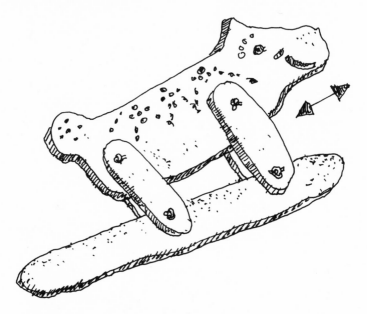

To work the puppet, shake the stick back and forth.

The recipe makes several stick puppets. You can double it if you wish. Stick puppets are a fairly ambitious project and you will get better at making them as you make more of them.

Variations

Try making simple marionettes out of gingerbread and licorice. Experiment with different designs, including insects that have more than two sets of legs. Figure out a way to decorate both sides of the gingerbread.

5

Molding and Casting

Molding and casting are techniques for reproducing three-dimensional forms. They do for sculpture what printing does for drawing. You learned the principles of molding and casting the first time you filled a pail with moist sand, turned it over, and removed the pail, creating a perfectly formed cylinder. The pail was the mold and the sand was the casting material.

In industry, molding and casting are very important processes because they create products that are uniform. Manufactured plastic goods, from toys to thin films to furniture, are mass-produced from molds. The bodies of automobiles, spacecrafts, and ships are cast from molten metal. Molding and casting have reduced the time needed to construct skyscrapers, bridges, and roads. So many items you use every day are made by these processes that it's fun to look around and see how many different molded items you can name.

To an artist, molding and casting serve another purpose than just producing uniform products. Artists use molding and casting to transfer their work from one material to another. For example, many great works of sculpture were first modeled in clay, a material that is easily modeled but very fragile. Plaster molds were made of the clay and finally bronze was cast in the plaster molds. The result is sculpture that has detail and variety of form easily accomplished in clay but also has the strength and permanence of bronze.

Casting and molding techniques are no strangers to food preparation. Molds for custards, cakes, jellied salads, cookies, and pasta can be inexpensively purchased at housewares departments. Cake decorating sets and cookie presses are also easily obtainable. Any of the recipes in this chapter can be used in commercial molds. But it's just as easy and much more fun to find molds in unlikely places or to make your own.

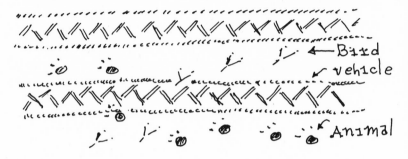

SPRINGERLE COOKIES: PRESSED MOLDING

A footprint and a tire track are good examples of pressed molding. An object that has a sculptured surface (a *template*) is pressed into a soft material, leaving behind a three-dimensional impression. A traditional material used in pressed molds in the kitchen is springerle cookie dough. Templates for these cookies can be purchased in housewares departments. They are usually carved in wood and are often in the form of a carved rolling pin which rolls the impression into the dough.

We, of course, didn't use the standard springerle cookie molds but found our own templates which we think looked just as good. Our friends had a hard time guessing what we used to make the designs.

springerle cookie dough (recipe below)
waxed paper
flour
rolling pin
sharp knife
small flexible spatula
large wooden board or flat plates
various templates such as:
    a potato masher
    a slotted spoon
    cut crystal (we used a plastic tray from the dime store that
       looked like cut crystal)
    nuts and bolts (well washed)
    Legos or other formed plastic toys
    molded bottles
    silverware handles
    dishes with relief patterns

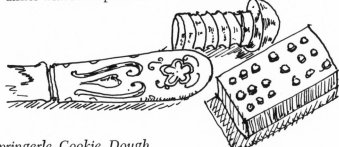

Springerle Cookie Dough

2 eggs
1 cup sugar
2 cups sifted all-purpose flour
½ teaspoon baking powder
½ teaspoon salt
anise seeds

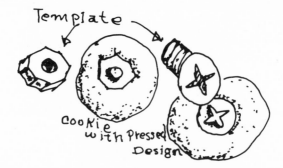

Template

Cookie
with Pressed
Design

Beat the eggs with an electric beater (if you don't have one use a rotary egg beater) until light and fluffy—about 5 minutes. Continue to beat the eggs as you slowly add sugar. Continue beating for another 10 minutes. The mixture should be thick and very pale yellow.

Resift the flour with the baking powder and salt. Turn off the beater and add the dry ingredients to the egg-sugar mixture. Mix together at low speed to form a stiff dough. (Note: This stage can also be done by hand mixing.) If the dough collects in the beaters, increase the speed so it spins out.

PROCEDURE

Spread about ½ cup of flour on a sheet of waxed paper and coat the rolling pin with flour. Roll out about one-third of the dough to a thickness of ⅓ inch. If the dough sticks to the rolling pin, scrape it off, knead it into the rest of the dough with a little more flour, and roll out again.

Prepare your templates by making sure they are clean and dry. Dust them with flour. Press a template into the rolled dough and remove to leave an imprint. If the dough sticks to the template add more flour to the dough or refrigerate for a few hours.

Cut the imprinted dough with a floured knife to form cookies. Lift the cookies gently from the waxed paper with a knife or spatula and move them to a board or plate. Let them dry overnight, uncovered.

The next day, preheat the oven to 300°. Grease cookie sheets and sprinkle them with about a tablespoon of anise seeds. Put the cookies on the sheets and bake about 15 minutes or until they are completely dried.

Variations

Other foods that lend themselves to pressed molding include liver pâté, gingerbread dough (see p. 62), and ice cream.

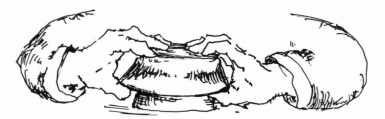

MOLDED MEAT SPREAD SALAD: PACKED MOLDS

Perhaps the type of "casting" easiest to do is the technique used with moist sand and a pail. The "casting" material is packed into a mold and retains the shape of the mold after the mold is removed.

There are many meat spreads that are suitable as casting material for packed molding. These include sandwich spreads of deviled ham and liver pâté. The challenge in this project is in finding unusual molds.

We became excited over the discovery of clear plastic "bubbles" that are laminated to cardboard over small items for sale in hardware and dime stores. We made a collection of the molded plastic packaging found on spools of thread, plaster anchors, and fish food.

Wash and dry your molds and pack them with meat spread. Refrigerate until well chilled before removing the mold by gently stretching the sides as shown.

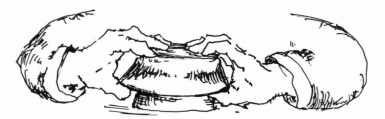

Arrange the molded meat on a platter with carved radishes (p. 92) on a bed of lettuce. Serve mayonnaise on the side and fresh bread and butter to complete the meal.

FRUIT JUICE BOMBE: COLD-SETTING MOLD MAKING AND CASTING

Many materials, including wax, chocolate, water, and gelatin, change from a liquid to a more or less solid state when cooled. While in a fluid state, such materials take the form of their container and retain this shape upon becoming a solid. You can take advantage of this property to make a mold of ice in your freezer and use it to form a frozen dessert.

a plastic football or large rubber baby ball that has a textured
    surface, or a small inflated balloon
an aluminum foil pan that is larger than the ball
vegetable oil
pastry brush
hammer
water
fruit juice bombe (recipe below) or ice cream

PROCEDURE

The first step in this procedure is to make a mold of ice.
Since water expands as it becomes ice, don't make a mold
out of anything made of glass. The pressure of expanding
ice can easily crack glass. We found that a simple form
made of inflated plastic or rubber works best.

Paint your ball or balloon with oil. Put it in the aluminum
pan and add enough water to come halfway up the side of
the ball when you hold it down so it doesn't float. (We held
our football under water by leaning a frozen leg of lamb on
it.) As the surface of the water freezes, the object will be
held in place.

Rubber or Elastic Bands

Let the ice freeze overnight. The next day pull out the object, leaving behind a perfect impression. Balls and balloons work well because you can squeeze them to remove them from the ice.

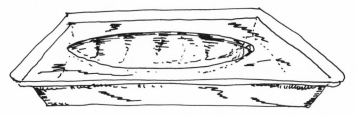

Pack your mold with ice cream or fill it with a fruit juice bombe (recipe below). Let the dessert become solidly frozen before attempting to unmold it.

To unmold your dessert, turn the mold and pan over on a plate. Remove the aluminum foil pan by pulling out the sides. Crack the ice mold by tapping gently with a hammer. Pull off the pieces of the cracked mold.

Fruit Juice Bombe

1 teaspoon unflavored gelatin
2 tablespoons cold water

¼ cup hot water
2 tablespoons sugar
1 cup fruit juice or mixed fruit drink
½ cup heavy cream, whipped

Put the gelatin into the cold water to soften. Add the hot water to dissolve the softened gelatin. Add the sugar and fruit juice. Chill until the mixture thickens but is not yet firm. Fold the whipped cream into the thickened gelatin. Folding is mixing very gently so as not to squash the air bubbles in the whipped cream. Cut down into the mixture with a rubber spatula and bring the unmixed part up from the bottom, turning your bowl a little with each stroke. Pour into your ice mold and freeze until solid. Freeze any remaining dessert in another container.

CAKE DECORATIONS: EXTRUSION MOLDING

A cake decorated for a special occasion is as much a work of art as it is a tasty sweet to end the meal. The elaborate scrolls and flowers of icing have been created by one of the most basic molding methods—extrusion, in which a soft material takes on form as it is squeezed through a hole and lands on a surface. You are familiar with extrusion molding if you use toothpaste.

Standard equipment for cake decorating is a pastry bag (which acts as a toothpaste tube) and a set of metal tips with holes of various shapes. Sometimes the bag is not made of fabric but is a metal or plastic cylinder with a plunger. You can buy a set at hardware stores or housewares departments.

You don't have to have a fancy commercial set to get artistic results. Here's how to make your own extrusion molding kit using scissors and brown paper.

MATERIALS AND EQUIPMENT

decorative icing (recipe below)
iced cake or cupcakes
brown paper
scissors and tape
waxed paper
small spatula for filling icing bags
toothpicks (for correcting mistakes)
paper cups
spoons
food coloring

Decorative Icing

¼ lb (1 bar) sweet (unsalted) butter
1 box confectioners' (powdered) sugar
1 teaspoon vanilla
1–2 tablespoons milk

Beat the butter until soft. Beat in the confectioners' sugar. Add enough milk to make a thick paste. Beat in the vanilla.

79

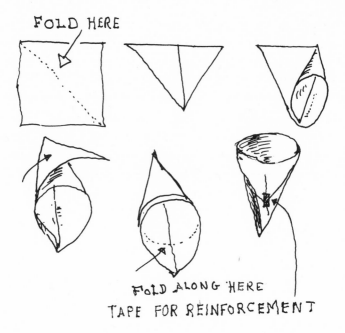

FOLD HERE

FOLD ALONG HERE

TAPE FOR REINFORCEMENT

PROCEDURE

Cut out a 9-inch square of brown paper. Fold it along the diagonal. Place the triangle on your work surface so that the crease is away from you. Bring one tip up to meet the point of the triangle but do not crease. Instead, turn the tip under and hold with your thumb against the triangle. Pick up triangle between your thumb and forefinger. Fold the other half of the triangle around the first half and secure the tip under your forefinger. This forms a paper cone with a tightly rolled tip.

Fold over the ends you are holding and tape them down to hold the cone together. Make several cones, as you will use each one for a different color icing.

Cut the tips of your cones to make different shaped openings. Cutting straight across will produce a round design. One notch will produce a leaf design. Two notches produce stars.

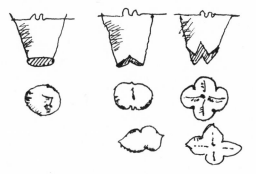

Before you try to decorate your cake, practice making icing designs on a piece of waxed paper using uncolored icing. You can then return the icing to the main batch, color it, and use it on your cake.

Push several tablespoons of icing down into the point of a cone. Fold the open end over several times to close. Squeeze and guide the cone with your right hand and steady it with your left. To make long lines, move the cone slowly while squeezing with a steady pressure. To make stars, use a cone with a notched opening, holding it straight up and down. Increase the pressure so that a small amount of icing piles up in one place. Remove the point with a strong motion so the icing breaks off.

Before you start plying your craft on a cake, plan your design on a piece of paper. Separate the icing into paper cups, coloring each batch a different color with drops of food coloring. Stir each cup with a different spoon.

Variations

Extrusion molding can be used for many other kinds of foods such as mashed potatoes, sandwich spreads, and cream puff dough. If you would like to make designs that require a larger opening than you made for icing, you will have to make something like a cookie press.

Get two paper cups the same size. Press down the rim on the bottom of one paper cup. This cup will be the "piston" of your press.

Cut a hole in the bottom of the other paper cup in one of the patterns suggested in the drawing. Fill this cup three-quarters full with soft food. Squeeze it through the opening by pushing down with the "piston" paper cup.

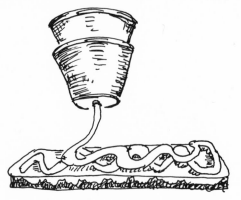

One kitchen tool that is perfect for extruding soft material is a garlic press. The tiny holes will form many fine threadlike shapes that make interesting designs out of extrudable foods.

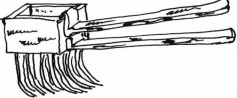

CHOCOLATE LEAVES: TWO-STEP DESIGN TRANSFER

One of the advantages of making molds is that you can make copies of fragile objects. In the next project, you first make a plaster mold of a leaf which can then be used over and over again to create leaves made of chocolate.

MATERIALS AND EQUIPMENT

newspapers
a round aluminum foil dish
a perfectly formed leaf that is smaller than the diameter of the
    dish (we used leaves from avocado plants and begonias)
vegetable oil
plaster of paris (from a hardware or paint store)
aluminum foil pan for mixing plaster
plastic spoon
sharp knife
aluminum foil
double boiler
high quality bittersweet chocolate candy bar
scissors
paper plate
pastry brush

Spread newspapers over your work surface. Fill the round aluminum foil dish about two-thirds full of water and pour it into another dish where you will mix the plaster.

Smear oil on both sides of your leaf and place top side down in the center of the empty foil dish. The underside with its pronounced veins will be up.

To mix the plaster, gently sprinkle dry plaster over the water until it no longer sinks beneath the surface. (You will probably add about twice as much plaster as water.) Mix until smooth with a plastic spoon. Pour the plaster over the leaf and let set until hard.

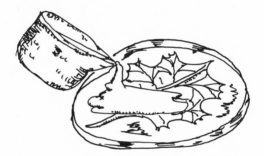

Note: When cleaning up *do not* pour unset plaster down any drain. Wait until it sets, then pour off any excess water and throw out hardened plaster in the trash.

To unmold your plaster cast, stretch the sides of the foil pan so that the plaster plaque drops out. Gently pick out the leaf by lifting it with the point of your knife. It doesn't matter if the leaf is destroyed. You should have a perfect impression of the leaf in a very smooth surface.

Your plaster cast will act as a die from which you can emboss (press) the impression many times into aluminum foil. Place a piece of foil over the impression and rub your fingers over it so that the leaf design emerges. Prepare several pieces of foil this way.

Melt chocolate over boiling water until soft. Paint several coats of melted chocolate over the leaf impressions on the foil and refrigerate until firm.

When thoroughly chilled, cut around the leaf outline with scissors and peel off the foil. Use chocolate leaves to decorate cakes, cookies, and ice cream.

6

Carving

Carving is sculpting by subtraction. Material is removed, leaving behind desired shapes and forms. Carving is a challenge to artists because there is always the danger of removing too much. Yet, despite its difficulty, carving is an important craft because it permits sculpture to be created out of materials that cannot be softened enough to be molded or modeled. Carving is the only way to produce sculpture in wood and stone.

Certain foods, such as vegetables, cheese, and chocolate, are ideal materials for learning the craft of carving. They are firm yet soft enough to cut easily with kitchen cutting tools. You can practice your carving skills, eating your chips and mistakes. Then someday you may use these skills to create sculpture out of more permanent materials.

CHEESE INTAGLIO

Sculpture that is set against a background and is looked at from only one side is called *relief*. Perhaps the easiest kind of sculpture to carve is a relief where a design is drawn with carving tools. Shapes and forms are hollows and grooves below the surface of the background. This kind of sunken relief is called *intaglio* (pronounced intal'yo). To get the feel of carving techniques, do the next project where you carve an intaglio relief in a piece of cheese.

MATERIALS AND EQUIPMENT

a block of hard cheese such as cheddar, American, or Swiss
wire cheese cutter (optional)
carving tools:
    small paring knife
    potato peeler
    skewer
    serrated knife
    pointed can opener
    fork

Before you try to make a design, practice using your tools on one side of the cheese.

The can opener can be used to make V-shaped lines. Use it as you might use a pencil.

The paring knife can also be used to make V-shaped lines. Draw, holding the knife at an angle. Make another cut next to the first, holding the knife at an opposite angle so the two cuts meet to form a V-shaped groove. You can also use the paring knife to remove large areas and make hollow shapes.

A skewer is good for making narrow U-shaped grooves and for making textures.

A fork can create interesting textures and patterns.

The tip of the potato peeler can be used as a gouge to make U-shaped grooves. Be careful not to dig too deeply. If you press in too hard and remove too much with one motion, the edges of the groove will not be sharp.

When you have finished practicing, make a design on the other side of the cheese or make your practice surface even with a wire cheese cutter. If you use Swiss cheese, make the holes part of your design.

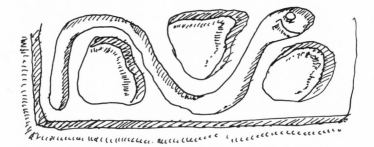

Variation

You can inlay your intaglio relief with a sandwich spread or cream cheese. Make your intaglio fairly deep with very sharp edges. Spread the inlay material over the entire cheese, filling the hollows. Use a wire cheese cutter to remove a layer off the surface, exposing the cheese as the background with filling as the inlaid design.

RAISED RELIEF

Raised reliefs are the reverse of intaglios because the backgrounds are lower than the sculpted forms. The drawing can be slightly above the surface of the background or forms can be strongly undercut so they appear to be almost free-standing against a "wall" of background. One reason why artists like to work in relief is that they can sculpt a composition that would be physically impossible if the sculpture were free-standing. They can, for example, include flying birds in their design. The background is the support for the bird. Since reliefs can be viewed only from one side they have been used extensively to decorate buildings and walls.

You can use any of the foods we mentioned earlier to carve raised relief. A thick block of cheese is probably the best place to start. Draw your design first with a skewer. Outline the forms with a paring knife slanted *away* from the design into the background. Remove the background carefully and slowly.

If you wish, you can cut all the way through the block of cheese, making the background into a hole. To make the remaining forms into rounded shapes, pare off thin layers of cheese until you are satisfied with the shape that remains. If you try to take off too much all at once you may go beyond what you want.

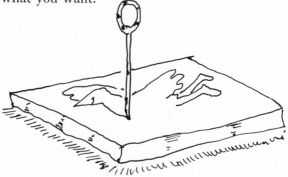

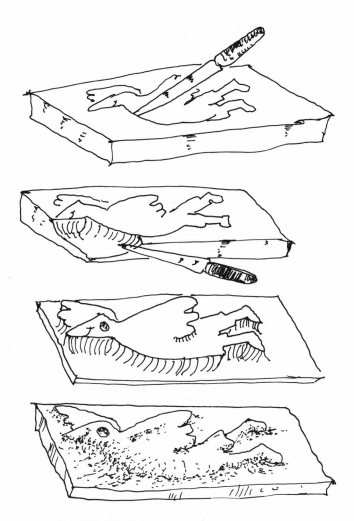

VEGETABLE GARNISHES

Caterers, who prepare food for special occasions, use carved vegetables as decorations on all kinds of fancy dishes. The carving often takes advantage of the natural shape of a vegetable and turns it into something else.

washed radishes, celery, carrots
paring knife
cutting board
toothpicks
potato peeler
bowl of ice water
bowl of salt water

PROCEDURE

To make radish roses: Make petals by cutting slices through the side of the radish as shown. Leave the slices attached near the base. Make five or six petals. Remove the red skin inside the rose. Soak in ice water for several hours to make the petals open.

To make more elaborate radish roses: After cutting a row of petals, shape the inside flesh so that it is a smaller version of the original shape of the radish. Then make another row of petals around this shape. Reshape the inside flesh and if possible cut another row of petals. See illustration.

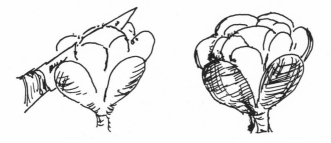

To make radish chrysanthemums: Slice off the top third of a radish. Use a paring knife to make many small parallel slices about ¼ inch deep on the flat white surface. Turn the radish and make another set of slices at right angles to the first set. Soak the "chrysanthemum" in ice water so it opens and "blooms." Use toothpicks as stems if you wish. You can also carve flowers from white radishes and beets.

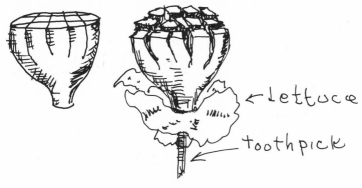

←lettuce

toothpick

To make celery curls: Cut 4-inch lengths of cleaned, washed celery. Make slits about 1½ inches long at each end as shown. Soak in ice water. The cut ends will separate and curl.

Note: FOR Best Results keep slices thin (one END of celery curl)

To make a carrot chain: Use a potato peeler to peel a carrot. Cut a length about 2 inches long. Use the peeler as shown to cut a slice of carrot. Lay the carrot slice on a cutting board and cut a hole at each end and a waist in the center with the point of the paring knife. Make a number of slices like this. Each piece will be a link in a chain. Soak the carrots in salty water for about an hour so the links become limp.

CUT AWAY FROM YOURSELF!

To assemble the chain, insert a link through both holes of another link. Pull the ends together and insert a third link through the two holes. Continue as shown in the illustration. Fasten the last link with a crosswise slice of carrot that you have cut into a ring with an opening.

Soak the chain in unsalted ice water to make crisp again. Use the chain to decorate a salad.

CARVED CHOCOLATE

Chocolate, like paraffin wax, is a material that can be carved as well as cast in a mold. You do a little of both in the next project, casting a solid chocolate block to be carved when cool, using both heated and unheated carving tools to create different effects.

One of the nicest things about carving chocolate is the delicious chocolate chips that are a by-product of your artistic endeavors.

8-ounce chocolate bar
double boiler
rubber scraper
5-ounce paper cup
paring knife with a wooden handle
waxed paper
other carving tools, including a potato parer and a fork

PROCEDURE

Melt the chocolate over hot water. Pour the melted chocolate into a paper cup. Use the scraper to scrape out the pot. Refrigerate the chocolate several hours until firm. (You can speed up this process by putting the chocolate in the freezer.)

When the chocolate is cold, peel off the paper cup. You now have a solid block of chocolate ready to carve. Work on waxed paper with kitchen carving tools.

Make head first; attach curls later

Chocolate can be nicely worked with a heated carving tool. Put the blade of a wooden-handled paring knife in boiling water for a few minutes. Rest the sharp edge of the hot knife on the chocolate and see how easily it cuts. Keep heating the knife in the boiling water as you carve.

You can make chocolate curls by paring the block with a hot potato parer. Later, you can set the curls into chocolate you have softened with a hot tool.

Try making interesting textures with a hot fork.

If your chocolate gets too soft as you work, refrigerate it until it is firm again.

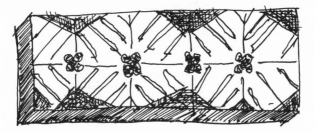

KOHLRABI MONSTER AND OTHER VEGETABLE BEASTS

Kohlrabi is a vegetable somewhere between a cabbage and a turnip. The leaves attach to an edible bulb in a way to inspire an artist. At least they inspired us.

MATERIALS AND EQUIPMENT

kohlrabi
carving tools
carrot and green pepper

PROCEDURE

Take a good look at your kohlrabi and plan how you will use the leaf attachments in your design. You can have the stems pointing up or down. You can carve holes to insert pieces of carrot or green pepper to add to your design. One of our kohlrabi creatures looked like this:

You can also slice off the outside of the kohlrabi, creating a cube of firm vegetable that can be carved into a piece of sculpture.

Variations

Many other vegetables lend themselves to carving. Try your hand at carving sweet potatoes, rutabagas, white turnips, and beets. Let the shape of the vegetable be the inspiration for the finished art object.

You can cook your sculptures and eat them later. Just boil them in salted water until tender. Add butter and seasoning to serve.

7

Assemblages and Constructions

One of the most striking breaks with traditional art is the use of "found" objects as art materials. Collages are pictures made with pasted bits of cloth, paper, feathers, and almost anything else that strikes an artist's fancy. Sculptures are made from welded kitchen utensils and other kinds of scrap metal or from glued or nailed items ranging from fabric to plastic to paper.

Art assembled from found objects can be as beautiful as traditional art but can also have a special meaning because of the materials from which it is made. For example, a piece of sculpture titled "Machine" that is made of welded pieces of wrecked cars may be one way an artist shows waste in our society. The artist's materials, found in junk-yards, are a product of human carelessness with machines built with hundreds of hours of human labor.

Foods come in so many different shapes, sizes, and colors that the possibilities for constructing and assembling food into art objects is almost limitless. The way a particular kind of food looks can suggest a piece of sculpture or part of a picture to you. Picasso looked at a toy car and saw the head of a baboon. He created a piece of sculpture where the car became the head with headlights as nostrils, the hood as the muzzle, and the windows as eyes. What do you see when you look at a pretzel or a carrot?

Assembling and constructing food into art is so much fun we did it at parties. Everyone brought a different kind of food to add to the collection of art materials.

OPEN-FACE SANDWICHES

Collages are pictures made of many found materials that have been cut and pasted on a flat surface. Slices of meat and cheese are the raw materials of the collages you can make for the next project.

sliced cold cuts such as bologna, salami, ham, and liverwurst
white and yellow American cheese slices
bread slices
black and green olives (optional)
pimiento (optional)
butter knife
scissors
cookie sheet
spatula

PROCEDURE

Butter one side of a slice of bread and place the buttered side down on a cookie sheet. With scissors, cut out the cheese and cold cuts and arrange them on the bread to make a design.

We decided to make faces. Sometimes we cut out the meat to make hair and used one color cheese for the face and another color for eyes, nose, and mouth. Other times the meat was the face and the cheese was the hair. We also used pieces of olive and pimiento to make features.

Put your collage under the broiler for a few minutes so that the cheese melts and all the pieces of the design fuse together. Remove with spatula.

SNACK FOOD SCULPTURE

The enormous variety of snack food, ranging from crackers and bread sticks to potato chips, pretzels, and corn chips, can be as complete a set of construction units as a manufactured building toy.

A group of us spent a rainy afternoon pasting snack food together with cheese spreads. We made space ships and sea monsters, washing down the imperfectly formed art materials with plenty of soda. The prize construction was a car that had a chassis built of pretzel sticks on an A-frame design. Onion rings were its slightly flat tires and rippled corn chips were its fenders. An extra pretzel served as its aerial.

at least four different shapes of snack food:

> We found snack foods can be divided into those that are structurally sound, such as bread sticks, pretzels, rippled potato chips, corn chips, cheese curls, and crackers, and those that are decorative, such as popcorn, potato chips, pinwheel-shaped snack food, and puffed flakes.

cheese cement (recipe below)

aerosol cans of cheese spread (optional)

a knife

paper plates

Cheese Cement

Soften a 3-ounce package of cream cheese. Blend in three tablespoons of sour cream and ½ package of dried onion soup mix. (This recipe can easily be doubled.)

PROCEDURE

Before you start pasting snack food together with cheese, it's a good idea to try to select and lay out the pieces you will be using as the framework of your project. If you wish to make a structure that has some height, use structurally sound foods like bread sticks as a "skeleton" and see if it will hold up for a few seconds before you start building. The cheese does not add to the strength of the structure.

It only holds pieces in position. Here are some examples of more solid structural frameworks made of bread sticks and crackers. Add decorative snacks to turn them into anything you wish.

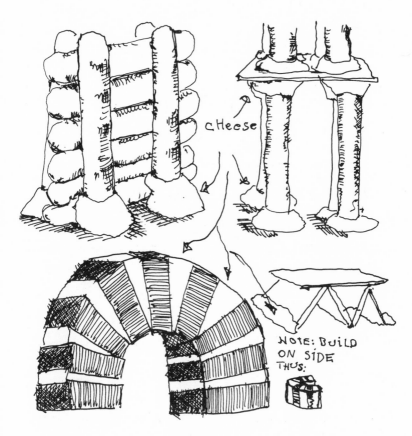

cHeese

NOTE: BuiLD ON SIDE THUS:

EDIBLE NECKLACE

No arts and crafts book would be complete without at least one jewelry project. You can make a bead necklace using shoestring licorice as your string. Beads can be dry cereal and hard candies with holes in the center. Or, if you wish, you can make your own beads by modeling and baking gingerbread (see pp. 62–67). Decorate gingerbread beads with cookie decorations.

Stringing edible necklaces is fun to do at parties. You can eat your finished necklace while you are wearing it. Just bite off a bead while being careful not to sever the licorice string.

PASTA MOBILE

People who work in arts and crafts long ago discovered pasta, spaghetti and related noodles, as an art material. Pasta is made of a high-protein flour that has great structural strength. Pasta comes in a variety of shapes and you can also get some containing spinach which makes it green.

We found pasta a good material for creating mobiles, hanging sculptures that move. You can, of course, put pasta together as traditional craftsmen do, using string and glue which make it inedible. We figured out a way of putting uncooked pasta together so that an art project can be dumped in a pot and cooked. It is completely edible except for any dust you may let accumulate on its surface.

MATERIALS AND EQUIPMENT

spaghetti
other pasta, including manicotti, lasagna, fusilli, ziti, elbow
    macaroni, bow egg noodles, shell macaroni
a large nail
pliers
paste of flour and water
knife
salt
colander
saucepan

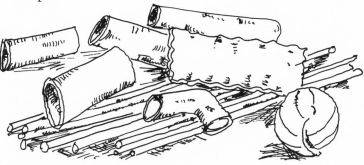

PROCEDURE

The techniques involved in assembling uncooked pasta require some dexterity and practice. It is helpful to have a plan of where the pieces will go before you start trying to put them together. Choose something simple for your first project.

The main method of attaching one piece of pasta to another is by tying them together with cooked spaghetti.

In order to tie pieces of pasta together, you will have to make holes in them. Hold a large nail by the head with a pair of pliers. Heat tip of the nail over the burner of your stove. Hold the pasta in your hand as you burn a hole through it or rest it on a surface so that there is nothing underneath the pasta to interfere with the nail as it comes through. Reheat the nail as necessary.

RIGHT   WRONG

Note: *The nail gets extremely hot so be very careful not to burn yourself.* You can't hold the nail with your fingers as metal conducts heat and the end away from the burner will get very hot.

A piece of lasagna with a number of holes in it is a good starting point for a mobile from which you can hang smaller pieces of pasta.

To cook spaghetti, put a handful of spaghetti in a large pot of boiling salted water (about a teaspoon of salt). Cook until tender or about 15 minutes. Drain in a colander and rinse with cold water.

make hole larger than spaghetti so mobile can turn

hooked ends like knots made when spaghetti is limp

flat surfaces will catch air currents and give movement to the mobile

Cooked spaghetti works very well as string but there are some tricks to using it. To pass spaghetti through a long tube such as macaroni or ziti, wet the inside of the tube to make the threading process easier. Dry off the spaghetti before trying to tie it, as sticky spaghetti holds a knot better than slippery, wet spaghetti. Be gentle yet firm when tying knots. If you pull too hard the spaghetti will break, but if you make the knot too loose it will come undone all on its own.

You can also attach one piece of pasta to another with flour and water paste. Simply add water to a small amount of all-purpose flour until it is sticky. Pieces will remain in position only after the paste dries so you will have to wait if you are attaching more than two pieces together.

As your finished assemblage dries, the cooked spaghetti will return to its rigid, uncooked state. If you hang pieces with cooked spaghetti, be sure to put your work in the proper position before leaving it alone to dry. If you wish to eat your assemblage, put it in boiling salted water and cook until tender. Serve with spaghetti sauce.

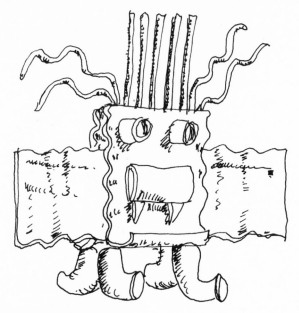

STRUCTURES IN SWEETS

The cooking style often considered the greatest in the world is French *haute cuisine* (pronounced ote kwee-zeen, French for "high style of cooking"). The father of French *haute cuisine* was Marie Antoine Carême (car-em), the chef of King George IV of England and Czar Alexander I of Russia. He was known as the "cook of kings and the king of cooks."

Carême wrote volumes on proper preparation of many now well-known dishes but his main area of expertise was desserts or confectionery. The desserts he created were such spectacular works of art that they often served as table decorations for large banquets. Carême thought of himself as an artist, a master builder, when it came to putting a dessert together. He said, "There are five fine arts: painting, sculpture, poetry, music and architecture—whose main branch is confectionery."

The next project is to recreate a dessert that made Carême famous. In many ways it is much like building with blocks. The "blocks," which you make yourself, are tiny cream puffs filled with whipped cream. The base of the construction can be a cake or a pie crust made of vanilla wafers. The structural support comes from sugar that has been cooked long enough to form hard candy threads upon cooling which crunch when you eat them. In fact, the dessert is called *croquembouche* (croak-om-boosh), which is French for "crunch in the mouth." It is truly a dessert fit for royalty and is one of the more ambitious projects in this book.

Note: The temperature to which the sugar must be cooked is well above the boiling point of water; that is VERY HOT! You should have an experienced cook supervise the cooking and handling of the sugar syrup part of this project.

First make the cream puffs.

Cream Puffs

1 cup sifted all-purpose or gluten flour
½ cup butter
1 cup water
1 tablespoon sugar
¼ teaspoon salt
4 eggs

Preheat the oven to 425°. Grease two cookie sheets with butter. Measure out your flour.

Put ½ cup butter, water, sugar, and salt in a small saucepan and bring to a boil. Continue boiling until all the butter is melted. Remove the pan from the heat and quickly dump in the flour *all at once*. Beat the mixture with a large spoon until a dough forms, a large lump stuck to the spoon. If the lump doesn't form right away, cook over a low flame while beating until it does form.

Let the dough cool slightly. Add the eggs one at a time, beating well after each addition with an electric beater. When you first add an egg, the dough will be in small pieces. As you continue beating, the dough becomes a satiny and glossy batter. Finished cream puff batter should be smooth and shiny and hold its shape when dropped from a spoon.

Drop by half teaspoonfuls on greased cookie sheets. You should get about 48 cream puffs. Leave about 1½ inches between puffs as they expand during baking.

Bake at a high heat of 425° for about 10 minutes, then turn the heat down to 350° and continue baking for another 25–30 minutes. Finished cream puffs are golden brown with rigid sides. They should have an even puffed shape that doesn't change on cooling.

Remove the puffs from the cookie sheets with a metal spatula. Let cool on a cake rack before filling.

Caramel Candy Structural Lattice

Note: *Now* is the time to call the supervising cook.

Put 2 cups of sugar in a heavy iron or enamel pot and heat over a medium flame while stirring with a *wooden* spoon. (Wood does not conduct heat and there is no danger of the handle getting too hot.) Continue heating this way until all the sugar has melted and is golden brown in color. This process of melting sugar is called *caramelizing*.

Remove the pot from the heat. SLOWLY and CARE-FULLY add ½ cup of water. Since the caramelized sugar is very hot, the water will start boiling as soon as it comes in contact with the sugar. If you add water too fast, there is danger of spattering.

Stir the mixture until the caramelized sugar is completely dissolved and boil a few more minutes until it is a thick syrup. There will be many small bubbles all over when the mixture is finished. Set aside and allow to cool enough to be handled but not so much that it hardens. Keep the candy soft while assembling the dessert by placing it in its container over hot water.

The dish should be assembled shortly before serving. You can build your structure on top of a plain round cake or in a vanilla wafer pie crust (follow the recipe on a box of vanilla wafers) or, more simply, in a pie plate.

Fill each cream puff with whipped cream from an aerosol can of whipped topping. Insert the nozzle of the can downward into the cream puff and press to fill. Or you can use real whipped cream. Use a pastry bag with a metal tip to fill the puffs.

After you fill each puff, dip it in the caramel syrup. Make a circle of about 15 cream puffs as a base. Build the structure by sticking on cream puffs in smaller and smaller circles until the structure comes to a point.

1. fill cream puff

2. Dip puff in caramel

3. First layer of puffs

4. Two layers of puffs

5. Project completed and decorated with pulled taffy flowers

You can embellish your croquembouche by drizzling any leftover caramel syrup over the structure and topping with a bouquet of pulled taffy flowers (p. 53).

Separate cream puffs with two forks to serve. This is one dish where it's hard to decide which is more spectacular—its taste or its looks.

8

Garbage Recycled as Art

Many foods have inedible parts. In the process of preparing food we often remove skins, leaves, stems, and roots. Other foods we eat first, leaving behind pits, cobs, and bones. Usually the inedible parts of food wind up as garbage.

Since this book deals with the creation of art in the preparation of food, we thought it might be fun to do some projects where art is created from the by-products of food preparation and eating. Although you won't be able to eat the projects in this chapter, somewhere along the way you can eat something related to your creations. We wouldn't want you to waste good food for the sake of art!

ORANGE PEEL POMANDER

A pomander is a mixture of good-smelling things made to hang in a closet. Oranges and cloves give off a spicy fragrance and have long been used to keep clothes from smelling musty. Cloves are stuck through the skin of a whole orange which is hung on a string and allowed to dry. We created a variation by using only orange peel.

MATERIALS AND EQUIPMENT

an orange
whole cloves
sharp knife
colored string
scissors

PROCEDURE

Slice the orange in half and pull out the pulp. Work carefully so you don't tear the peel. By pulling out the white membrane you can completely free the peel of pulp.

Cut shapes out of one half of the orange peel. We made circles, stars, and crescents. Cut the same shapes in reverse out of the other half orange peel.

Fit two similar shapes together so that the white sides are inside. Hold them in place by inserting cloves from both sides. Tie colored string between peels around a clove to hang.

Hang several different shapes together. As they dry over the next few days, they will give off a pleasing scent and become smaller in size.

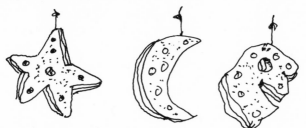

PEACH PIT RING

You don't need any special tools or setup to make rings out of peach pits. All you need is a peach pit and some rough pavement or a file.

Rub a curved side of the peach pit against the pavement until you expose the soft spot near the center. Rub the other curved side the same way. Poke out the soft center and you have made a peach pit ring.

If you make a collection of peach pit rings, you can string them on a ribbon to make a belt.

Peach pit rings are fun to make on a summer day when you have been eating peaches with friends.

SEED JEWELRY

Different kinds of seeds can be strung as beads to make attractive and unusual necklaces and bracelets.

MATERIALS AND EQUIPMENT

seeds such as pumpkin, squash, watermelon, cantaloupe, popcorn, dried beans
paper towels
colander
needle
nylon thread
pliers
long, thin finishing nail
hammer
old wooden board as a work surface
varnish or clear nail polish (optional)

PROCEDURE

If you use seeds from fresh vegetables or fruits, wash them with running water in a colander and pick them over to remove fibers and pulp. Spread the seeds on paper towels in a single layer to dry. Dried seeds can be given a shiny finish, if you wish, with a coat of clear nail polish.

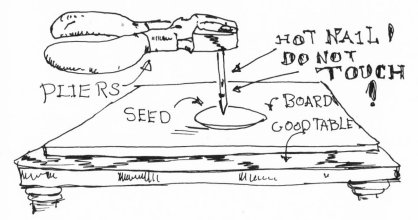

Make holes in the seeds before you string them. You can hammer a hole (which sometimes causes the seed to split) or you can burn a hole. Use the pliers to hold the head end of a long, thin finishing nail over the burner of your stove. Press the hot tip of the nail into the seed which is resting on an old wooden board. If you do the hole-making operation on top of a good table, you can easily damage it as the nail comes through the seed.

Use a double thread, the desired length of the finished necklace or bracelet, and a needle to string the seeds. Experiment with making different patterns using seeds of different plants that are different sizes, shapes, and colors.

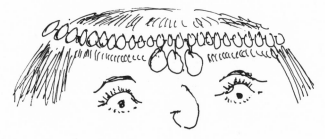

WALNUT SHELL MARACAS

Walnut shells can be turned into percussion instruments that add their own special sound to folk and rock music.

MATERIALS AND EQUIPMENT

walnuts
cherry pits
a slim, sharp knife
all-purpose glue
ice cream sticks
rubber bands or small C clamps
varnish or clear nail polish (optional)

PROCEDURE

Open a walnut by slipping the knife between the two halves of the shell and prying it apart. Remove the nut meat and the stiff, fibrous material inside the shell. Scrape or file the base (the flatter part of the shell) so that when the two halves are fitted together there is a space large enough for the insertion of an ice cream stick as a handle.

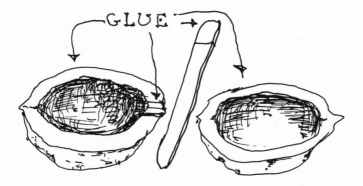

GLUE →

Spread glue all the way around the rim of one half shell. Also put glue on both sides of the end of an ice cream stick. Place a cherry pit in one half shell. Fit the two halves together with the ice cream stick as a handle. Wrap a rubber band around the shell or clamp with a small C clamp to hold the maraca together for 24 hours until the glue is dry.

If you wish you can varnish the finished maraca or paint it with enamel.

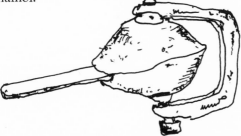

BUSHY-TAILED CORN HUSK ALLIGATOR

Corn husk dolls are a common craft project that is part of American tradition. We used some of the same techniques to make a corn husk doll, then turned it upside down to make a most unusual creature.

MATERIALS AND EQUIPMENT

fresh, green ear of sweet corn
paper towels
scissors
string

PROCEDURE

Remove the husks from an ear of sweet corn, being careful not to tear them. Wrap the husks in wet paper toweling to keep them moist and flexible. Cut one husk into thin strips that will be used to tie the body of the alligator and the ends of the braided legs.

Remove a bunch of corn silk which will be the tail. Surround the corn silk with five or six corn husks, their curved surfaces facing out as shown in the picture. Tie them tightly in place, about ½ inch from the end, with several wraps of string.

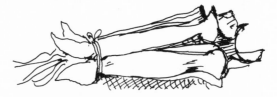

Fold the corn husks down over the string, revealing a tail of corn silk. The string is now on the inside of what will be the alligator's body. Tie a "waist" with a strip of husk about 1½ inches from the tail. Tie a second piece of husk an inch from the first tie to form the neck. Trim and push the ends of the corn husks to form an open alligator mouth. If you wish your alligator to have hair, slip some corn silk under the neck tie.

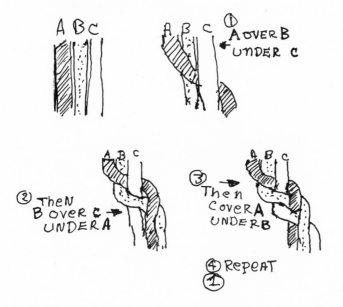

To make the legs, cut a corn husk lengthwise into three strips. Tie the strips together at one end with a strip of corn husk. Make a braid 1½ to 2 inches long and tie with another strip of husk. Trim both ends. Slip the braid through the body to make legs as shown in the picture. Make another braid for the second set of legs.

Make a small slit at the top of the head near the neck and insert a short folded strip of corn husk as eyes.

Bend your animal into a standing position and allow it to dry for several days.

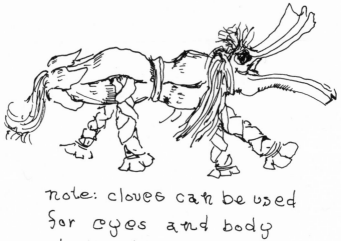

note: cloves can be used for eyes and body decoration.

About the Author

VICKI COBB received her early education at the Little Red Schoolhouse and attended the University of Wisconsin on a Ford Foundation Early Admissions Scholarship. She earned a bachelor's degree from Barnard College and a master's degree in secondary school science education from Columbia University Teachers College.

Mrs. Cobb has taught general science and physical science at Rye High School, Rye, New York, and at the Manhattan Day School in New York City. She is the author of several books for young people, including *Science Experiments You Can Eat* and *How the Doctor Knows You're Fine*.

About the Illustrator

PETER LIPPMAN holds degrees in art history and architecture from Columbia University. He has also studied painting and drawing at the Art Students' League, and bronze sculpture and casting in Madrid. He has both written and illustrated numerous books for children. His other work includes encyclopedia articles, animated television commercials, illustrations for many national magazines and the *New York Times*, and sculpture, drawings, and paintings that have been exhibited in the East. Mr. Lippman's illustrations also appear in *Science Experiments You Can Eat*.